THE NOW

Pitt Poetry Series

Ed Ochester, Editor

THE NOW

ALBERT GOLDBARTH

UNIVERSITY OF PITTSBURGH PRESS

Published by the University of Pittsburgh Press, Pittsburgh, Pa., 15260
Copyright © 2019, Albert Goldbarth
All rights reserved
Manufactured in the United States of America
Printed on acid-free paper
10 9 8 7 6 5 4 3 2 1

ISBN 13: 978-0-8229-6593-0
ISBN 10: 0-8229-6593-3

Cover photo: A visitor in the Pont d'Arc Cavern in France. Courtesy Idealink Photography /
Alamy Stock Photo
Cover design: Joel W. Coggins

for Skyler: in the now
(and the always)

———————

in memoriam,
Michael Cissell

CONTENTS

———————

Autobiography: 1947 / 2018

Coda

NOTE

While none of these poems was written to fit (and certainly not to be limited by) an organizational formula, in hindsight two communities declared themselves.

The first section asks to be sensitive to a future that increasingly on a daily basis colonizes the present moment . . . although our technology changes so rapidly now, my "present moment" in writing this is no longer yours in reading it.

And so in content, and sometimes in presentation, these poems— no matter their immediate subjects—are colored by an awareness of multicongruities, info overload, data economies, "cloud" storage, conflicting realities, online mind-meld, fluid truths, layered identities, neural rewiring, etc., and the kind of connectedness that's both an enabling new power for our species *and* a world of outsourcing human importance to new, nonhuman extensions. Well, "new," in any case, as of the shelf-life date below.

The second section asks to remind us that for futures to be born, pasts need to die: these are poems that mark (often that eulogize) disappearances, from people to artifacts, to loves, to certain cultural sensibilities and our memory of them . . . from species extinction to divorce court. (Although occasionally losses are restored.)

Perhaps the book's intention to find an uneasy triangulated balance among the vanishing past, the shaky present, and the onrushing future is implicit in its coda poem, where "digital" is *both* physically anatomical and incorporeally virtual. Even as I write these few lines, someone somewhere is excavating real bones from the ground of real colonial Jamestown; someone is running the stats from that through an algorithm. Where we live is that nano-moment between: the now.

September 2018

THE NOW

———

THE BOOK OF ~~TOMORROW~~ TODAY

Winston Churchill said about architecture that "we shape our buildings, and afterward our buildings shape us," and the same is true of the Internet.

Andrew Blum

Rhapsody at the End of Human Language

My old phone, hooked up, transferring
its data to my newly purchased phone
through some impossible intermediary
data-share device: in the future

this will be "sexual intercourse," this
will be "job" and "government oversight."
When I see the future coming toward me, *zoom*,
it isn't coming toward me,

it's here. And even that idea, that new idea,
is already old. If I'm correct in this, then everything's a cliché
as soon as it's uttered—and saying that serves

as its own example. Which is to say . . .
if time is actually a construct in our minds, it's now
a different time than ever
and our minds are different minds.

In fact, if time is known
by linear and progressive change,
there isn't time any more,
just simultaneity . . . as in

This bird ~~was~~
          is

—as soon as "happen" occurs, it's reoccurred
into its next tense. So this poem is both
the end of human language *and*
a traditional lyric poem. In the latter,

that bird from six lines up
is a brooch, a scarlet brooch, on the velvet
deep green breast of the forest.
(That's the way we'd say it ~~then~~

now.) The sun confirms its constant presence
at the tip of an inhuman-scale distance
by the slats of light the rustling
forest canopy admits into the otherwise

consistent gloom of this afternoon
in this forest near the snow line.
Enter the bird, so quick, so blur-quick,
it reminds me of when Robert Bly ~~wrote~~ writes

We are the sparrow that flies through the warrior's
Hall and back out into the falling snow.
and this image of evanescence
is so beautiful, so beautiful

that I want to cry out, "Bird,
thou art a churning of the air
as if you could thicken it
into something richer. Stay a while,

be not so ready to flicker and disappear!"
—the way that it was spoken,
without self-consciousness, without irony,
once upon a time when there was time.

My Friend Dayvon, a Flying Saucer Enthusiast (Read: "Nut"),

is googling "ufology," you know, the study
of "unidentified flying objects," but
—his finger's too-quick tap—"urology" pops up.
Although I've only experienced one of the two
(my urine still reveals a ghostly blush
of blood sometimes, a brief reminder of the surgical
reduction of my prostate that thankfully
saved my life) I understand how –ologies
blend or overlap confusingly: moreso now,
in a googleverse, than ever. In an early letter,
writing of dawn, when he normally worked, the poet
James Wright observed, "There is something uncluttered
about the air at that time of day," and I think we all
have a sense of how used the air can come to feel,

———————

entering our lungs after having dragged across
the –ology of torture (someone staring with her one eye
at the other eye, on the dirt floor, gelid, beginning to lose
its spherical definition by now) and the –ology of carnival
on the fireworks, snake-dance, booty-beat streets
of Rio . . . maybe it's this one woman accentuating
her already mucho hypnotico eyes
with butterflies of sparkle paint that has me
flipping back and forth confusedly between
those two completely unalike domains and the breaths
of their participants. You know: the way they always say
in science magazines that any breath you take may hold
a remnant molecule of Jesus, Elvis, Cleopatra, the zither-playing
busker on the corner, that dog you buried in 7th grade . . . they

———————

mix and remix in your pulmonary welcoming
of oxygen, they jockey for attention in your mind. If
one night Jesus zithers "Blue Suede Shoes" and "Hound Dog"
in your dreams, it's understandable enough. I even think
it's understandable that one day I was floated
into a lit arena, on my back, surrounded by alien beings
in robes and masks, and another mask was set
on my face, and then their alien probe-things
entered my body, their incomprehensible science
entered my body, in an otherworldly wedding of hurt and healing.
I remember that I tried to be brave, whatever
this –ology was. I tried to be strong and not break.
"The branch will not break," as James Wright wrote.
I might have inhaled at atom of him.

This Age of Terror

In Borough High Street, south London,
on April 21, 2016, the local police responded
to a call about a "suspicious package"
left at a bus stop. Such, after all,
are the times in which we live. It could be
any person attempting to board the plane,
it could be any ordinary bunged-up piece
of Wal-Mart luggage. What if the woman positioned
to smilingly high-five the first of the marathoners
breasting the line has a wired palm
and doesn't mind dying herself? Such are
the times, and their stories. In Italy,
in the city of Modena, the local police
were called about a rubbish bin

suspiciously buzzing, and the bomb squad
set up a 200-meter cordon and went about
its gingerly business for three fraught hours.
It's tempting to wax imaginative—"the sky
above that bus stop was a school of fish-bone clouds,
to which the setting sun provided a lush
and appropriate salmon color"; while "the sky
above that rubbish bin was as clear (the Italian
saying goes) as a baby's initial tear, as clear
as a glass of white wine made from grapes
(the saying goes) pressed only by toes of virgins."
Tempting: "the onlookers milled about like a battery
building up voltage," etc. But no: these need to be
factual in the telling, so that

their final moments also follow through as true. Because
it's increasingly difficult—it *is*, for all of us—to know how

to maneuver through the overwhelming facts out there,
or pseudo-facts, or cyber-altered "news."
The bomb-smoke footage of invasion: do we panic, or do
we roll our cynical eyes? When is our gauged reaction
adequate, and when is it a mismatch? When they
tell her—all too suddenly, there in the clinical
iceberg light of a hospital hallway—that her mommy is dead,
what squeaks out from her seven-year-old's body is
a titter, is that first attempt to dial across the wavelengths
for a fit. In movie audiences, too:
the default titter, when the poignancy onscreen is too
enormous and naked. So this, I see, has become a poem

that considers our misplaced responses to cues,
even as it's about assumptions and objects
that are also misplaced. The sandwich in the brown bag,
for example, that released a misty spray of egg and pesto
all over the nearby first-floor windows, when
police in Borough High Street necessarily conducted
a controlled explosion. Sometimes it *isn't*
a bomb. Sometimes this age of terror skews
our expectations out of reality. In Modena, they discovered
at last that the sinister buzzing under the rubbish
came from a tossed-in vibrator. We can guess
at the hearty duration of the onlookers' spasms of laughter.
And it's tempting, of course, to join them in that;
as if this were a funny poem.

Deep Down

I have said, and intend to say, nothing of the hideous business of the Six Snowmen, and the unspeakable end which threatened Ursula Trelawney.

Cay Van Ash

Okay, let's count 'em up. There's 1)
a small-time pimp with big-ass dreams;
2) an undercover op [as opposed to the undercover cop
he sometimes sleeps with]; 3) the newbie dancer
at Titters; 4) the nurse in the refugee camp,
in a never-ending pinwheel of sweat flies; 5)
the undercover cop; 6) the top-floor CEO of the very
important multinational petro-corporation that . . .
what *does* it do, exactly, and does even the embedded
exposé reporter have an inkling?; 7)
the single mother with her two jobs, one of which
I can't reveal; 8) the exposé reporter. But
I see now that my numbered list misled you
into believing there are eight people. No,

there are four; but each is two of the list, and some
are even more than that, although we'll never know just
who and which, no more than the one-sixteenth-of-an-inch
of a knife-tip broken off in the body of one of these people
—carried (dull and inert and inoperable, a bad dream
with a mineral weight) in a deep-down muscle—
will ever lead back to the knife itself, or the forge
of its birth, or the story of the attack, which is,
by now, not even a hinted-at glint on the bottom
of a lake of changing seasons, screening weeds, and too much
intervening time. No more than anybody's—yours too—
2.5% Neanderthal genome is going to declare a visible,
you-could-point-your-finger-at-it presence: but it's there,
deep down, in the species bud. The National Security Agency

(Fort Meade, Maryland: *sssh*) "each year
obliviates one hundred million supersecret documents"
[I think I'll repeat that figure: *One Hundred Million* a year]
—these papers are driven at sixty m.p.h.
through turbine "suck pipes," are converted by a hydro-pulper
to "grayish slurry," and then are sold for their reconversion
as pizza boxes, egg cartons, grocery bags: the tales
that may have toppled governments (or rescued them) are blotting
lipstick, swiping clean a dipstick, are as unknown
an unknown as the year in a cult for one of the eight
(who are four). And I'll tell you one has jail tats, but
inked where only one of the other four will ever see them
and excite them with the drag of a hungry tongue. As for that year
in the cult: one night, a dozen couples in an octopussish,

orgiastic writhing in the "Meditation Pool"; another
night, the damp "Interrogation Cellar," there
without food or a light, although the rats saw perfectly well.
How *could* that astonishing history ever be erased! And
yet, it's erased. The eight (who are four) are here
at a party; its raucous surface is dizzily busy
enough without the past. "Hey everybody, look!"—the trick
with the shotglass and the egg. The standard acoustic
wrestling: country, rap, in alternating strangleholds.
Some arguing. Some flirting, maybe serious, maybe
just to stay in shape. Hot Slicez delivers: pepperoni.
The paper towels below the greasy heap of onion rings.
The pizza box, that once was the story of Ursula
Trelawney, six imposing "snowmen," and . . . other things.

One Definition of Time

She was photogenically pretty—so important
if media coverage is intended to last—and young; and
so her death (her crimson Volvo skeetered over ice
and into the river) became the point
from which her life was retroengineered to fit
the needs of either 1) the "scandalous" (with that,
you'd think her days were spent entirely
at the strip club, Baby-O's: where its infamous
"VIP Room" promised the hungry media gossips
endless opportunities for seedy speculation) or 2) a brand
of secular saintliness (the volunteering at Rest Care Manor,
the Children's Urban Literacy Foundation Drive: again,
the sense was these entirely represented her energy
and hours) . . . but of course when we step back in Time

(as any science fiction story demonstrates, or
there isn't a plot) we superimpose, it might be
with the innocence of chrono-tourists casually
lollygagging about the 19th century ("Look!
A butter churn!") or might instead be with the conscious
agenda of altering the "flow of events" ("With luck,
we'll downtime in Washington on April 14, 1865,
just moments before he exits the carriage
with Mrs. Lincoln. . . ."); either way, Time,
in its travel from the Big Bang
to the farthest eventual fadeout rim of Expansion, is
an ever-forward impulse, and refuses backward
tampering. An entire subgenre of science fiction
posits unflagging Time Patrol detectives, alert

for the glitter of pop tops in the muck of the Paleozoic,
for a button-size spy camera in the grand salons
of gold rush San Francisco . . . then they try to smooth
that fourth dimension wound. Of course our minds
don't have such vigilant constabulary;
offer us the chance to reinvent ourselves "back then"
as heroes, or (sometimes the rewards are as great for this)
as victims, and the past . . . ah, but there isn't any "the past"
as a singular construct . . . no, there's really
as many pasts as there's us. One example here
would be the downy cloud of her breath
in the alley, laughing with Thick and Dazzle the way
that people do at 3 a.m. with one last Jack-and-Coke,
and then the snow-on-brickwork crunching as she teeters

to the Volvo, and the small clicks of her three attempts
(the last a success) to slip the fucking key in the ignition.
The moon in the clouds is where the sun's light goes
to draw up the sheets and sleep for a while. The road
is smooth—or "slick" perhaps, but "smooth" is how
she feels it, smooth and accommodating, and
friendly, and so the sudden uncontrollable skid
at the river bend isn't only unexpected, but a betrayal
by the elements of the night. Her eyes
try to fly from her face like terrified birds and,
if there's a nest, if there's a tree, in this metaphor
I'm inventing, it's the long and languorous floating
of her blonde hair in the water, for the three days
that it takes before her sunken car

is discovered and reclaimed. All this,
however, is only a story I've forced
against the grain of whatever "actuality" is (or maybe
the verb is "was"). Time doesn't care about the beauty
of my language, or our noblemost intentions,
or about the reshaped history we use
as validation of our grabs for power here and now.
I'm sorry, do-gooder, generous-hearted casters
of Broadway hits and flops, but there were never
sheriffs in the Old West, never any Roman senators,
who were black. There *were*, however, "Negro cowboys"
(some think 10%): their absence from the t.v. Western dramas
of my childhood is a milder—but still regrettable—
version of Stalin's well-known "unexisting"

of his political foes: murdering them, well sure, but
then also erasing their ever having been. Anachronism,
then, is not only a positive—those pop tops—but often
a negative space as well. I think I'm trying to suggest
one definition of Time is "integrity."
Thirty-four seconds after the title credits
of John Ford's *Cheyenne Autumn*, a Western
set in 1878, we can see,
and it's shocking, it's a wrongness, streaks
of jet contrails crossing the heavens. They're
lovely, though, the way that things grow lovely
even as they disappear.
I think I'm going to name them
after her dancer name, Skye Bleu.

gO

1.

On the astral plane, the astral citizens feel completely
corporeal—they leave grapevine trails
of bruises, or the sexthrill scree of gooseflesh,
on each other's skins—but to us, of course, they're
barely shapes of the kind of thickened air one finds
over mineral springs; *they* must call *us*
the creatures of the astral plane, may think of us
(if ever) as translucent kites their own, more "real,"
lives fly by a string of interdimensional connection.
Meanwhile, the aliens who colonized Earth originally
are applying their "people-look" makeup over their scales.
Meanwhile, a diagram of all of the ley lines mapped so far
reveals that Stonehenge is situated to act
as their "nexus of power," like a pimple ready to burst.
One day many years ago I asked my wife what heaven
might be like. "I think that everyone gets the heaven
he believes in," she breezily said. We both thought it
silly. Now I've come to see that reality is like this
too: we live in the one we believe in. So the wife
believes her husband is faithful. The husband believes
the child is his. It works. One day their house is suddenly
vacant. I believe they moved together from Phoenix
to Ohio. Ollie believes they disappeared through an opened portal
into one of those space-time tubes that tunnel the universe.

2.

Ohio, as it turns out (this is obviously *my* version of "real,"
not Ollie's), is much like Phoenix, since this couple is much
the same as they were in Phoenix, and our *who* is so often
the major sensibility determinant of *where*. The woman is
stretched out on a lawn chair in their yard, is like
the mould of an ingot slowly filling with gold light
that the sun, on this day the weather channel calls "partly sunny,"
pours down; in a while her final shape as an object
of precious glowing value will be attained.
The man is practicing racquetball and every wham
off the wall he rewhams back is like, or feels like,
a symmetrical rightness added to the world,
a little system of worked-out anger and expert accuracy
that moves the planet—his planet—around as smoothly
as the Earth in a well-oiled orrery. At the same time, she
partakes of the look of a goddess on an ancient,
half-ruined obelisk overrun by jungle creepers, and so
is moving a certain undisclosable prophecy one more stage
toward its completion. At the same time, he repeats
and repeats a mystic pattern (the wall and his serve
are like call-and-response in a church service) that recalibrates
the axial tilt of the world. Well, if there is "a" world.
The dowser's willow wand dips onto the planet's skin exactly
where, on its other side, the dark, fantastic "hollow Earth" takes over.

3.

Or not fantastic—not to its populace, for whom a day
of continent-carving floods and travel by teleportation is ordinary.
Also metaphor ("like the mould of an ingot," "like
a symmetrical rightness"), no matter its first, ostensible
purpose, always implies that a life is never
one thing. At the airport today, we're encouraged to cheer
for Reynold, a frail, pale "Make-A-Wish" kid on his way
to a weekend in Disneyland . . . I can't begin to imagine what
he'll undergo one day when the monster simmering in his marrow
boils out . . . and I suspect (he's six) that, blessedly, neither
can he. And at the same gate is this fashion model,
Starr, whose biggest worry is keeping her nails from chipping
—"Although I've had it tough. When Ace and me were in our 'weed days,'
we were *so* poor we'd tear pages out of [she lowers her cat-purr voice]
a Bible to use for rolling papers." These are citizens
of cosmic realms as distant from my own as those of the Yeti,
Leviathan, Merlin, Gorgon, Swan Girl . . . though with them,
as with Reynold and Starr, a whispered back-and-forth ventriloquy
occurs in my brain before sleep comes on. The snazzy
in-flight magazine has a story on ballerina Misty Copeland:
"the plutonic ideal of fitness." Right idea, very
wrong reference; and an example of how the mythic
intrudes upon our everyday discourse in the unlikeliest of ways.
A "dream" is another word for "concurrency."

4.

Osmosis: two-way travel across a membrane. It's
because that kind of permeable borderline is common
in the multiverse, that Nessie, and the saucer people,
and levitating yogis sometimes leave their ho-hum everyday existences
for ours, where they're flamboozingly extraordinary. Our mouths,
our eyes, go wide and round in a semiotic for "wonder." But
then, a sunset also does this—it's the love-child of an ember
and a rose today, I think I can almost hear it hiss
as it's doused out on the horizon—and certain favorite poems,
and the way my wife will hum to herself in performing
mundane tasks, as if the folding of laundry were somehow
a physical counterpart to musical composition and determined,
fold by fold, the release of notes. It must be wonder is where
we look for it. It must be that a Swan Girl
who's invisibly attached to my wife by a wiffling, occult cord
of etheric sisterhood looks into our house from her swan nest
far away and is gogglingly mystified by her glimpse of something
this marvelous: laundry! humming! a sun of grand
blood orange effulgence! But that's getting a little too goopily
supernatural. In the "real world," that couple has moved
again, from Ohio. To where? To right here. It isn't
accidental all four sections of this poem begin with a capital "O,"
a space-time portal. They've tunneled through the back of this poem.
They're here—a moment only. Given their wanderlust, they're ready to
gO.

Wrist Beep

Once there weren't even cell phones,
hard though it is for a twenty-something
to credit that—but I remember those days,
and we communicated fine. Now, of course,
there are phone/computer/location chips
the size of a grain of rice
you can have implanted in your wrist.

In the detective novel, the wisdom is
don't bother to trail your mark from behind;
he'll be checking over his shoulder
especially to see if he's being followed.
If possible, stay a little *ahead* of him.

If that's how it works I think I get to say
the future is stalking me.

A Work Week of Muchness

By 900 A.D. over 20 "holy sites" throughout Europe
claimed to be the repository of Jesus's foreskin.
Catherine of Siena claimed His prepuce was
her "heavenly wedding ring." Leo Allatius (c. 1586–1669),
Keeper of the Vatican Library, speculated the foreskin, like
the rest of His body, ascended—freighted with the numinous,
weightless as dandelion fluff. / When the automobile
—the "horseless carriage"—was still a rare
and a luxury item, high-dollar brothel harlots
would dab a hint of gasoline behind their ears
and under their arms. / A dazzle of mating
dragonflies: like watching the light itself break into,
and out of, an intricate scrimmage. / The ancient Egyptian
mummifiers are known to have mixed,
for expediency, a dog's paw or a bird's claw in with human
bones; and sometimes, after the gun goes off,
you stand there staring dumbly at this alien thing
your hand has become, metallic and smoking. / The 7:
Wonders of the World, Dwarves, Ages of Man. /
Italics always seem to me like letters
a breeze is lightly tilting. One thinks of the O's as a bicycle
in the Tour de France, leaning into a curve. /
Escrow. Pi. The speed of light. / *How can the world*
contain all of this? How can a brain survive
in such a world, in such a muchness?

"She would stay up on the roof all night"—of
Caroline Herschel, who discovered seven comets;
her second, just before Christmas of 1788,
was moving across the constellation of Lyra—the "Lyre" or "Harp"—
as if (this is my fancy, not hers) it were performing
its contribution to "the Musick of the Spheres." / HAIKU:
Seventeen people on a street corner:

    cop siren:

empty corner. / Another fancy: a raven in flight,
gulping down some morsel that was rising up
in front of it. How long would it take
for that everyday bird to develop a nimbus around itself,
having ingested the foreskin of Christ? / Absinthe;
that woman; fossil fuels; that man: why
are we drawn to what destroys us? / Charles Babbage's
and Ada Lovelace's "Difference Engine No. 1"—essentially
the first computer, in 1837—was designed to require
25,000 brass cogs. / Kimono. Dashiki. Zoot suit. Prom dress.
Burka. Surplice. Sweats 'n' hoodie. Longjohns. Sari.
Burka prom dress. / Oak has a density
of 750 kilograms per cubic meter. / The Chickasaw (OK)
newspaper: Jay's Jewelery: "Buy an engagement ring.
Get a free shotgun." / *Help me, I'm drunk,*
I'm drunk on muchness, I'm riven between its horror
and its inundating beauty.

French aerialist Jules Léotard developed
the flying trapeze in 1859—and of course you know
what else, by his name. The Australian acrobat
Unus could balance himself upside-down
on one finger. / My colleague Chris can tell you
what it's like to walk around with someone else's lungs
in your chest; although all of us walk around
with hard-working oxygen in our lungs that's been used
infinitely already. / Cyborg. Android. How many more
shiny new names will there be for the loss of our humanity? /
Thirty-eight syllables: the hummingbird *Calypta anna*
possesses thirty-eight syllables in its repertoire
of song. Its pippin heart can beat over a thousand times
a minute. / And what of the tree that became
the two crosspieces they hung Christ on—did it know,
did it grieve for its wooden children
the way that Mary, pregnant, might have intuited
what was to come? / Heroic readers: Harriet
Beecher Stowe, at age twelve, read *Ivanhoe* seven times
in one month. John Adams's copy
of Mary Wollstonecraft's milestone *Rights of Woman*
has 12,000 words—*12,000* words—of marginalia
thoughtfully quilled. / *It's here, and then more*
is here, and then more. The cosmos is unboundaried;
the mind is a valiant thimble.

Caroline Herschel preferred the relatively nimble 20-footer.
Her brother William, however, was proud of the 40-footer
(then the world's largest) and with its distance-power
began to envision what's now our 21st century understanding
of "deep space." Still, when its one-ton mirror slipped
from the casing, he was nearly killed. / How did
"Professor Porco" (as an 1890s circus poster
assures us) train his pig to play a robust, recognizable
"Yankee Doodle" on the xylophone? / *Fugu*, the puffer fish
in Japanese; one accidental taste of its liver
—or of any part of the fish the liver has touched—is fatal.
And so (we're such irrational creatures) the meat is considered
a delicacy—"cut so thin one could read
through the flesh." / Seeing the hummingbird's wingflaps
(if they can "be seen"): like watching the invention of invisibility
take place. / My friend Denton climbed the stairs inside
a statue of the Buddha so colossal that seven sightseers
fit in the head. "To be up there was like . . . like being
one of the Buddha's thoughts. I ran from ear to ear
a dozen times: the Buddha was feeling joyful!" /
"Mass-produced chairs, selling at 30 to 75 cents each,
doubled the number of chairs per household
from 1800 to 1830." / *"Information overload":*
I've known people who drowned in those waters;
yet other kinds of people sport like dolphins in those deeps.

God says, "Welcome, little one. When a hunter's arrow took you
in the dead of a moonless night, because you were glowing, that
was my Son in you—as He had as much of *you* in *Him*
as He did of the dove." And that's how the raven got into Heaven. /
Houdini practiced picking up pins *with his eyelids*. /
HAIKU: Corpse with a knife in its side
        —reminds you of bread.
And of our shelf life. / The H-bomb America tested
November 1, 1952, "had a force that was greater
than all of the bombs dropped in the two World Wars
combined." / "Escrow": will somebody please the hell
tell me what escrow is? / Birth: you trade in your placenta
for your shadow. / Those images of people—sinners—
in Hell: like the silhouettes of birds we tape to our windows,
TURN BACK NOW. / In 1962 John Glenn orbited the Earth three times
and in under five hours witnessed four sunsets. /
Sir John Herschel, William's son (and also "the greatest
astronomer of *his* generation") dismantled his father's
40-footer on New Year's Eve, 1840, "holding
a party inside it, with drinks and toasts and candlelight."
(What would *you* give to have been there?) /
Information noise information noise information noise:
the *real* ping pong / *I look in the mirror. It's*
me. I know it's me. And yet I know it's also
an integer of the Muchness.

A Talky Trip Through Mash-Up Time

1.

*By the time we get to the 2040s . . . computers will go inside
our bodies . . . we'll be online all the time.*
                                        "futurist" Ray Kurzweil

Goodbye, goodbye to the borders
of the self. Hello to . . . excuse me a minute,
a ganglia alert in my elbow is telling me
my favorite show on retina-vue, *My Synthesex*,
is on in a couple of . . . oops, shit, now my group-chip
is in hyper-jangle mode
with a psych-prompt *not* to watch it, where
was I? —Oh yes. Hello to a future
you may welcome enthusiastically into your human plasms,
but that I see as another invader
taking over the body, and then—goodbye—the species.
Just last year three friends of mine died
of the older cancer. Spare us this new one.

2.

At The Thirteen Stars, a colonial-style restaurant
"authentic in every detail," part of the charming authenticity
is that Thomas Jefferson serves our tea
and our red-and-white-striped flag-shapes of brioche, since
evidently the authenticity of having a Negro servant
deliver a platter of possum haunches met
with only mixed success. At least a dozen nouns
on the menu are preceded by "ye olde." When Jefferson
finally clears away the empty plates and returns
to the kitchen, giving Betsy Ross (or maybe Dolly Madison?)
a friendly whomp on her ass in passing (a style
of political *joie de vivre* that doesn't seem to have dimmed
with the passing of time), my friend leans in

and whispers to me, "He's dead, you know.
We've been waited on by a dead man." This encourages me

to share with her my off-the-cuff conviction that
in the very near future a television/web channel will be devoted
in its entirety to celebrity funerals—hey,
how could there *not* be, money and voyeurism being
our favorite marriage?—and that celebrities will cannily
pre-auction off the paparazzi rights, the way they do now
for their weddings and the births of their children,
their liposuction and drug addiction counseling.
By the time Ben Franklin sidles up with our sillibub
and a kindly gratis aphorism or two, I've managed
a segue into Kurzweil's edgy predictodomain,
although painting it in my own dyspeptic colors, so that
my friend says, "I don't think I want to live

to see that future." I agree: "Me too!" We clink
the rims of our authentically hand-blown, globby glasses.
The problem is, of course, that I'd like to be immortal.
Who *wouldn't?*—given lingering health enough, etc. In 1045 B.C.
the Chinese poet Fenghao wrote in an ode, "The doings of heaven
have no sound, no smell," and I do *not* find that
attractive. So that's a problem: not wanting to see the future
but wanting to live forever. And then I say, "Well maybe
I can be immortal *backwards* in time," and we start to laugh
at such an exorbitant, nincompoopish idea, and even
Franklin and the just-arrived-for-the-night-shift
Martha Washington, who overhear this, chuckle,
as good hosts will . . . but no one tries to parse out
what this *means*, "to be immortal backwards in time."
It *sounds* good, sure. But what it *means* . . . ?
I'll get back to you on that, as soon

as my wife turns off her Twitter badinage;
and my father-to-be turns toward my mother-to-be
below the alignment of stars in 1947 in Humboldt Park
and asks her if she'll marry him, with a tremulousness
in his voice like that of a glass of jelly set on the sill
while a coal truck rumbles past just yards away;
and Monet sets down his brush for the day, his eyes
like bowls that need to be emptied before any more
can be poured in; and Lincoln weeps; and Paul Revere
inhales the combo scent of his horse and his midnight speed,
and Washington looks at a hole in a young man's side
and weeps, and Jefferson walks alone in the dark lanes
by the slave shacks, feeling pride and shame and sex
and a love of architecture, and weeps; and the Grand Khan
formulates a witticism and everybody laughs,
and the wine is exhilarating, the loins are abuzz;
and the chests are filled with gold; and the corpses are thrown
like fish guts overboard; and a scribe is embellishing
roses onto the name of Christ; and a scribe is embellishing
fanned-out rays of sun around the Pharaoh's cartouche;
and the enemy host descends; and a swell of erotic pleasure
rises from the shadows in the trees; and the trees
are a single undisturbed majestic continent,
unto themselves; and the caves belong to the bears;
and the waters descend; and the planet is newly formed,
is vectors of energy searching for immanence;
and the energy is all there is, and "soon"
there *isn't* "is" or "isn't"; and the Big Bang
is a quiet door I open
and step out of.

THE BOOK OF DISAPPEARANCES

_Long! Nothing is long! The time will soon be gone and
we shall be surprised to know what has become of it._

John Adams, as quoted in his biography
by David McCullough

P. L.

1. *What Is It About Our Lives*

I'm *not* in a war zone, and I *don't*
have even a cold much less a condition
requiring tubes, requiring knives, and words
like "litigation," "overdose," "foreclosure"
aren't a part of my day . . . why can't we
ever find a pleasure in this, the real pleasure
of everything that could have happened
but none of it happened,
what is it about our lives that leaves us
always seeking Something
and unaware of the benediction of Nothing?

2. *The Hum*

To the snooty horticulturalist
whose hobby is breeding competition roses, the thorns
are nothing—are beneath
consideration. The florist
snips them. But as Phil Levine says
in one of his final poems, "thorns /
too need to live." They're as remarkable
a combining of sun and nutrient
as the sumptuous, mazey folds of the flower.
The nutrients need to live. Their atoms
need to live. The empty space that hums
between the atoms needs to be,
and is, the void in which potential waits
to be actualized. Or ask the poet:
the blank page clamors silently
to live, to live, to live.

3. *A Million*

Without the tunnel of nothing
and the holes of nothing in its roof,
the flute would have no music.
Without the zero, there wouldn't be
a million. "The music of eternity,"
Phil says in that same poem. The past
is always a fat, fat clutter of rats
and kings and cathedrals and battleships
but the future . . . is empty, the future
is the purity of nothing.

4. *When Frannie Was in Her Seventies*

What's an "old lady's" worth, amid the world's lush roses
of sexual ooh-la-la?
                                            Phil told me this story
once: He and Frannie were entering a subway car
in New York, when a dumbshit twenty-something brawler
shoved Frannie out of his way, to get onto the car
ahead of her. Phil tripped him,
                                            and the fuckhead
took a juicy, sprawling headfirst fall. He glared up
from the floor at my seventy-something, thin-as-a-stick
and bookish poet-friend and sneered, with its
implicit threat, "Hey! I *saw* you do that."
Phil looked down at him. "You were meant to."

5. *The Circuit*

"All that's left" (this is Phil again)
"are these few unread words
fading before your eyes." And then . . . ?
The empty air—that nothing.

And inside it, over the highest peaks,
the snow is created; and born;
and falls; and feeds the rushing melt
that flows in rivers
over the downslope plains—tributaries
of nothing, bearing nothing
into the great nothing sea.

It's like watching the circuit of someone's breath
entering through the empty O
of OMG, and then exiting
—for those inclined to believe this way—
through the G that created Everything.

for Wayne Zade
and Skyler Lovelace

I Never Do Read the Last Chapter

of biographies. The one where they die.
There's enough of that already, here,
where Robby's MS, after years, grew bored
of playing at cat-and-mouse
with his nervous system, and one day
while he was resting, it unsheathed
the blades of the death kit
in its paws, and severed the necessary
life-strings of his body; here,
where all of us watched the schooling clots
beneath Theodora's skin, like fish
that you can sometimes see under ice
when it's thin enough, when it's ready
to crackle and then disappear; and
here, where something—soul? the spirit?
ectoplasm? a "governing force"?—
strained, and persisted, and
freed itself, leaving Gary's body behind
the way the freed fox leaves
the gnawed-off part of its leg
behind in the trap. These recent instances are
prospectus enough; I don't require
a bigger reminder. I've had, like you,
that understanding—I think of the crimson stain
at the heart of a peach—imbued in me
since birth: it doesn't demand
reactivating. I don't need to discover
you can announce to the world the true
concentricity-shape of the solar system,
you can lead a ragtaggle group of the enslaved
to the North, to a free state, you can pose

your near-unearthly beauty in the photo shoots
that outwealth certain countries'
entire annual fiscal profile—*those*
are the chapters to read!—and still
the final page is an indifferent wind
rearranging the ashes. Why should I have to suffer
Monet's imposingly, monumentally, larger-than-life
accomplishments becoming life-undone?
In 1879, as Camille lay
on her death bed, he was "quite naturally
devastated," and even so, and all that while, love,
like a dampening watercolor,
bled into duty, and so as he sat there
studying "the fading colours," blue,
and then yellow, then gray, in a fatal
diminuendo, he paid his wife
an artist's honor, and sketched her
stilled and pallid face. Now fifty-seven years
ahead, *his* turn arrived for embodying
that palette. The light outside the room,
as if recognizing the great blaze
of himself fading down to embers,
shook, then dimmed. A moan escaped
his water lily ponds, a silky, low moan, but
they heard it as far away as the coast,
where onlookers saw the coracles on the water
rock elegiacally, mournfully,
back and forth, and a quieting patter of rain
—enough to shut one's eyelids, only that,
no more than that—descended
for a moment from a strangely cloudless sky,

and his body heaved once like a carapace
splitting open for something new
and unexplainable to rise up, and
the trumpets sounded,
the angels roared like beasts.
Or however it happened.

"John Adams just died," I announce

by way of explaining, when my wife asks why
I look so maudlin. And yes, that "news"
is out of date by 192 years in current-me-time
but (since, given the brain's own
googledimensional layers and the universe's
string theory multicongruencies, two contradictory
truths can exist simultaneously), in the pages
of biography-time that death is as fresh
—as moving—as the moistened eyes and quavery

hymnful voices of the 4,000 mourners gathered
at the First Congregational Church in Quincy, Massachusetts,
and, later that day (his body placed
where it had been so many nights: alongside
Abigail's) as fresh as Pastor Peter Whitney's graveside quoting
from the Bible, "He died in good old age,
full of days . . . and honor," which I can still hear
in the time machine spiral deep in my ear, and which
I bring back with me, vivid and echoing,

into 2018, from the mazes of my reading. It seems
there's a continuum we travel, where the living and the dead
cohabit, fluidly: and words like "ghosts" and "memories"
and (in science fiction) "wormholes" and (in fringe psychology)
"memes" or "past regression" attempt
in their inadequate way to explain why all the times
I fuck up (and they're frequent) my father is sadly,
fondly standing behind me, shaking
his translucent head in silent and translucent

resignation. If you don't believe this theory I'm proposing,
I can tell you that my friend Wayne Zade

phone-texted me when Dick Allen died, age 78,
a poet I'd never met but whom I'd been reading
with pleasure and admiration for all of my adult life
and who, from the little I knew, had always felt to me
to be a decent man, and true—in a modest,
non-trendy way—to the Buddhist sensibility
of his poems. A week later, I open the winter 2017

Gettysburg Review, with Dick Allen's bio note
in the present tense: he "lives
a stone's throw from Connecticut's Thrushwood Lake."
The poem (page 638) is titled (wondrous?
spooky?) "Back Among the Living": which he surely is,
of course, translucently. "You will never be alone
with a poet in your pocket.
You will never have an idle hour,"
John Adams ~~said~~ is saying.

James Madison as a Humming

*Having outlived so many of my contemporaries, I ought not to
forget that I may be thought to have outlived myself.*

James Madison

We think of them most ideally as a uniform force,
an original American "band of brothers," united
—just as the States were becoming—in hammering out
a gameplan for "democracy." But Adams said
of Franklin he was "malicious," "cunning," he
"will provoke . . . insinuate . . . intrigue . . . maneuver . . .
I cannot bear to be near him." Thomas Paine
was "a mongrel between Pig and Puppy, begotten
by a wild Boar on a Butch Wolf." Hamilton said
of Adams, according to Joseph P. Ellis, he was
"mentally deranged and unfit for the presidency."
Etc. They were heroic—but human. (The difficult
fact of slavery confounded them all.) We choose
to remember the heroism, to picture them working
in concert toward a noble end—and "concert"
is apt here: single notes in a grand
and overriding orchestration of political goals.
So that when only one remained (ironically
Madison, the most frail of them) he wasn't himself
so much as the lingering last sound
of a generation. Cue in blues musician
Henry Walker, circa 1955, playing
a Wichita club on Ninth Street, jammin', JAM-min,
lost in it, then suddenly . . . *a shot.*
"My guitar went twang, and I jumped off the stage.
I wasn't there, but my guitar was still humming"
—the way any spirit might still hum
for a little residual moment
when its body is suddenly gone.

There are poems about paintings, but the paintings are lost.

Guy Gavriel Kay

This is the way we know the sun at night,
when it's lost behind the rim of the world
—the moon reminds us. The moon is the sun
second-hand. So many of my poems exist
to commemorate the missing, sometimes explicitly, but also
the ones where my father is fixing snow chains
to the Chevy's tires, having scraped it out
of a ten-foot fall of December weather, like some eager
eighteenth-century archeologist hacking away
at Troy or Jericho; and my mother is contemplating
the mixture in her meat loaf pan as if
she's a pioneer woman surveying the waiting, patient
Great Plains; and the wall phone,
and the typewriter, and the mail box on the corner
have a currency that hums the air one-atom-thick
around them. Now they aren't here,
unless "here" is my words. There are statues of gods
from ancient Greece that we know of
only because of a play or scrap of prose description
that survived, in a jar, in the jaws of a mummy
—cast that way, like a shadow, into the future we call
the present. And the animals that hibernate—the small ones,
deep in their winter nests—that still their interior beat
to almost nothing, to a forgotten painting,
around which they curl
their outside body, the poem, that keeps it alive.

Lost

By the closing years of the twentieth century only one known asteroid was unaccounted for—an object called 719 Albert. Last seen in October 1911, it was finally tracked down in 2000 after being missing for eighty-nine years.

Bill Bryson

Does anybody wear "slacks" anymore?
Maybe. A few. A men's store
in Ottumwa, Iowa, is said to even have a sign
on a mannequin that advertises,
still, their availability. The radio there
is playing Frank Sinatra or Rosemary Clooney
—it's the great era of "crooners"—and someone
is saying "Whillikers!" Now that language

is about as lost—although I admit "about"
is very flexible here—as the words a woman
—"female" anyway, *Homo naledi*—chanted,
or shrieked, or whispered, when the corpse
she cradled against her breast was taken from her
for depositing at the thinned-out end
of the finalmost arm of the passage-maze
in the burial cave. Or . . . sang?

—because, like any of us, our crooners
must have had ancestors too. What sound
would have flowered out of my mother's throat,
in the maternity ward of Lutheran Deaconess Hospital,
when I was lodged in the swollen flesh
of the gateway, a breach birth
being pulsed by uterine forces against
an opening sized wrong for this aslant

debut? My father thought he might have lost
us both. He didn't. Luck and Doctor
Emanuel Kipnis saw to that. And *was*
whatever strangulated (and lightly medicated)
1948 *Amateur Aria of Pain and Glory* issuing
from my mother irretrievably gone, in the instant
of its release? Maybe. And yet the fine
preservatives of our undermind are loathe

to let their hoarded treasure perish—in the way
that the bones of *Homo naledi* (just look
at that hand we've rearticulated, it lusts to cup
a basketball!) remained whole in what we could call
the Earth's subconscious, deep by
two million years. Emanuel Kipnis scrubbed up.
He walked into that room,
and he rolled up his sleeves, and he hitched up his slacks,

and he dragged me into the future.

Walt Whitman, Barbara Bath

It's because the box I grab off the shelf
at Walgreens promises "antigravity" contents
that I start to think of birds,
those never-doubting, grand
ascenders, and then in particular (and this
story, says *BBC Wildlife*, is "well-documented")
the robin "a woman had taken
to feeding regularly on the sill of her open
bedroom window": one day, ill, unable
to step from bed, she woke to find
the bird on her chest "attempting
to feed her worms." It's what birds *do*
(for example, see Keats and Shelley): they lift
our spirits. And people successfully
disobey "the law of gravity" too, albeit more
laboriously, in their a-to-z
(that is, airplane-to-zeppelin) way; and
even your jump, my jump, and certainly some
Olympic hurdler's smooth leap is
a momentary defiance of the planet's
grip. Of course on the other hand, those zeppelins
would self-combust and crash; from far,
"I saw the very heavens
rupture, and hellfire light the skies," and
from close, "The screams
of the falling men still haunt me now,
years later, as well as the stench
of their roasting skin." We're fools
if we think we can rise above suffering
permanently. And still, we're so relentless
in silver-lining even our grimmest weather:
tending to the carnage

hauled in daily to the hospital tents
of the Civil War—the raw, foul sawed-off arms and legs
the nurses piled in barrels, some from victims
as young as fifteen—Walt Whitman held,
as if to a talisman, to the story a Northern soldier told
of how, when he lay wounded after a battle,
left to die on the frozen ground, a Southerner
came along on the third day, "bound up his wounds,
cheer'd him, gave him a couple of biscuits
and a drink of whiskey and water." And just yesterday
at the "visitation"—Barbara in her casket,
a gem of the mortuary arts: you'd swear
she might sit up and wink, which, after all
would be just like her—I found myself
half-believing myself when I said to her daughter Julie,
"Well, don't think of it as a time to mourn,
but to celebrate her life." So
when my nanosecond misapprehension passes
and I see that the toothpaste container
promises nothing more than "anticavity" . . .
still, I catch myself, for the rest of the day,
smiling through the weight of the usual dreariness
with a buoyancy.

Origin-Place

It makes good sense that universe
and uterus ask to sound alike:

all of that plush sufficience and total
surroundoenvironment, there

in the womb. And yet we're expelled:
here we are with our desks and mountains and heart-shaped beds

to prove it. The story of Eden must be
our almost, *almost* remembering

that origin-place . . . it's like the fingers trying
to play piano keys

through boxing gloves. "Born" in this version
of human existence is synonym for "exiled."

Some say crying
or inhaling, but

our first act on Earth
is forgetting.

Album

In this one, *circa* 1978, I have a 'fro
that's like the marriage of a poodle's coat

and a cotton candy machine. It isn't *styled*
so much as *globed*. In this one, earlier

by a little, I have a twisting jet-black
waterfall of hippie hair and a Nehru jacket

I wore because the male models in magazines
devoted to songs about flowers and peace signs

did. Did I say "poodle"?—in this one,
here he is, a miniature, Tuffy, I'm holding him

and sporting sideburns about the shape
of Florida. You know who's the greatest

comedian? Time. And every year of our precious lives
is the setup to one of Time's unfailing

punch lines. We can spiel all we want
about Time as the great democratic leveler;

healer of all wounds; destroyer; and all
of the other pieties and profundities that pour

forth from our storehouse of blah.
But Time's most favored gesture

is a startling, wry rebuke. It's
true. And in *this* picture the fashion is

to have a living mother; and father;
a first wife; and a sister with breasts.

Switch

From Lee Server's Pulp Fiction Writers: *"Trying to avoid two stories set on the same planet in the same issue . . . [Leigh] Brackett's editors once simply changed the title of [her] piece from 'The Dragon Queen of Venus' to 'The Dragon Queen of Jupiter.' . . . [In Horace McCoy's No Pockets in a Shroud] the editors . . . changed one female character from a communist to a nymphomaniac."*

One-night stands are perfect
examples. Seth recalls a woman who woke up
around three in the morning, padded to the balcony
bare-ass, and announced to his neighbors
in a voice of triumphant certainty, "I am Jesus
returned from the dead!" and then collapsed
in a chattering fit; while Lora remembers
the man—she never did learn his name—
who'd looked "so normal—normal and *cute*,"
who, after the sex, in the lazing, casually revealed
he was a vampire and politely requested, as if it were
a beer or a glass of tea, a tiny runnel of blood
from a razor-nick in her upper arm: he'd
thoughtfully brought the razor. Neither of these

received a second invitation, and in any case
were worth it for the story they provided—a kind
of dividend—over the years. But what about a decade's-worth
of marriage, and children, and only *then*, halfway
through year eleven, does C. decide that fulltime riding
with the Leather Bunnies Bikers is "more me" than volunteering
at the parish's Holy Community Counseling Center;
not to mention R. announcing to his family that
from now on he would be addressed as *Miss* R., now
was "commencing [his] life as a woman." Read these anecdotes
as sad, or brave, or risible: whatever, they're
the not uncommon afterfact of having personalities
susceptible to change—to what, in Brackett and McCoy terms,
is an unexpected editorial switcheroo. Don't children

understand this mind-plasticity
implicitly?—the parents with the comforts and the gifts
become the wielders of punishment, chaotically, completely
topsyturvily; how many of our fairy tales and horror movies
exist to enact this fear? How many senators in Congress
turn out not to be the people we thought we'd elected?
Werewolf, etc. Schizo office colleague, etc.
Give me a rock to cling to that isn't tomorrow's
sand. Give me a particle that isn't all itchy
to flounce about as a wave. You know the wish I mean:
walking under the thirty-personae moon,
invoking the wheel of stars as a witness,
the wheel of seasons, the wheel of evolution: *Give me
my original Venusian, the one I proposed to.*

I'm tired of my student Scott Galloway

being dead. I'm tired of him being thirty-nine
forever while everyone else, who cared for him,
is slightly different every day,
a few amazing splashes of pleasure
along a line of diminishment. There were twenty of us
at a beery wake in the back room at The Anchor,
with the laptop like a rear-view mirror—Scott
and Lisa, Scott with his eleven-year-old daughter
holding his hand—while the rest of us kept on
driving ahead, wherever "ahead" is. Tired
of remembering how gentle he was. And tall.
We read his poems out loud, but failed to get
the tall in. Sick of having to think
how what we are, how what we *really* are, is the revealing
of how chance works. Let's return to what
the rest of this city is gaga over: the vote on whether
to fluoridate our water, the vote on whether a casino
out in the county is a helpful peck of fun
or Satan's handiwork. It isn't easy to concentrate
on the wars and the scores and the recipes
when Scott has left the universe of nouns
to become a past-tense verb. I'm tired of trying to find
a way to say that; every way is inadequate. Flawed.
I'm plain tired. But I won't keep you in suspense
any longer. The vote is fluoridate no,
casino yes. By now those two ideas—the dental and the Vegas—
are married in my squooshy brain, and you
can kind of see the amalgam here,
an early evening crowd with *some* of the Boeing employees
working the slots with gritted teeth
as rigorously as they work the front-plate buffering line,
and the late-night dazzle of off-work strippers

spending the *other* Boeing employees' Friday checks
and flashing their perfect veneers. In the first few weekends
everybody in the city has been here, checking it out
at least once: what isn't,
we seem to be saying, a gamble? I'm sick of the 70-year-old man
who entered Dollar General looking for last-minute candy
to bring to his grandkids and left it like venison,
in a sheet, with a bullet inside his head, which makes
a simple errand a game of Russian roulette. I'm sick
of my sister's mastectomy, which makes our DNA
a hand of dealt cards. Sick of one friend's prostate,
sick of another's slowly occluding heart. Some nights
I read that poem of Scott's where the weight of everyone's frailty
added together only makes him feel more tenderness,
even for the orderly with the needle-tipped tube of dye.
Not me; I'm tired of these scenes in our poems.
I'm tired of being rendered to bones
as if this writing I love to read and love
to make myself is an acid.
These cancer poems, these AIDS poems,
don't forget the drive-by shooting ones.
What are we, in such poems?
There are nights I punch the pillow, as if that could help,
one-two, one-two,
and it continues in my dreams.
If this bed won't stop bucking,
how do I know I'm not dice?

Change

Everything does, and must—that's a condition
of being "everything," or even the smallest part of it.
The atoms of uranium are morphing
to the background beat of the Geiger Counter;
"the day" is letting its cornsilk-yellow slip
wriggle down to the floor, and is stepping out of it
as if from a pool, and is transformed
into "the night"; the words of the treaty
are becoming the actual, real-world results of the treaty
—a different thing altogether. I'm old enough

to remember the neighbor girl as five, in the yard
with grandma, learning weed from plant,
and giggling, running in circles . . . now the charges
are possession and soliciting, and the boyfriend's
worse: a knife is involved, "he's so *nice*
but the meth changes him to a monster." Ovid
knew these stories over two thousand years ago.
We should have a device called an Ovid Counter,
and then we could follow the upticks in its static,
a kind of sonic graph, as—some in punishment,

some in redemption—Io is transmogrified into
"a milk-white cow"; and Echo is discovered on his funeral bier
become "a flower of gold with white-brimmed petals"; Syrinx,
"a sheaf of reeds" and Myrrha, a tree (her thighs and belly
scaled in bark, her veins refigured as xylem and phloem
and, last, her weeping alchemized into the myrrh of the tree
that memorializes her name). Niobe is turned to stone:
"even her entrails." And the sadly misborn Iphis, as betokened
by her "unnatural cravings," becomes a man: "hidden fibers
seemed to guide her body." I'm old enough

to remember the slums that seeded the gentrifications;
yes, and the swankier streets that degraded to slums.
By now, we're bored with CGI: decent lawnmowing taxpayers
into zombies, in a digital flick of pixelwash. I'm
old enough to have suffered the bodies of friends—too many—
cancerously altered into otherbodies.
Perhaps the first "special effect" in movie history
(while accidental) addresses this. Mèliés was shooting
a street scene, and his camera jammed, then continued; when the film
was finally developed, he witnessed a bus turn into a hearse.

Makes the Beauty

It happens every year, why are we always so
amazed at this trick of a profligate bouquet
of carnelian-orange, mottled lower-register yellow,
circus and abbatoir cardinal-reds,
impossibly whisked from inside their boughs?
And yet we *are* amazed—perhaps because the tree
somehow is both the hat *and* the magician.
The leaves are so beautiful, it's hard to believe
they're burning inside, like monks protesting a war.
It's the dying—the dying so flamboyantly—
that makes the beauty.
The intel from photosynthesis central command
is the same, but the sugars are no longer up to it.
Even the word, if we let it float in the air
unbodied, is beautiful: Immolation. Immolation.
Soon, for its moment, each individual leaf
will float in the air, will pirouette
or gently rock like a coracle in a lazy chop of water.
Always down, though—bringing that last bright burning
into the earth, like a sunset.
When my neighbors wanted a ceremonial send-off
for the ashes of their cremated schnauzer, Renee, they
chose the back yard pit where the year before
we'd roasted a whole pig: drumming, dancing, chianti galore.
And so the commemoration was marbled through
with memories of the embers and the sweet slide
of the crinkled, blackened skin across the delectable meat.
In a couple of months, Renee indivisibly mingled
with that year's lush autumnal fall.
For the most part, dying's so gradual, so always here,
it's hard to draw a distinction; there are no

pure states. We've witnessed elephants
bring—by the trunkful, stately, repeatedly, until
the ritual task was completed—
leaves to scatter on top of their dead.

Fraud

Almost thy plausibility
Induces my belief
Emily Dickinson

The blackened glass nipples of Doctor Richelsbacher's
Supreme Magnetobody Rebalancer were buckled over
the neurasthenic's own nipples, and with the cumbersome aid
of a stiff cloth harness, rubbercoated wires the width of a fire hose,
and a console panel sized to the wobbles of battleships,
they reestablished "lines of healing electrolytic salts
throughout the body's humours," and sizzled, and fizzled—and he
was hustled out of town by the bunko squad and still

he set up shop anew with his Supreme Deactivating Gastro-Meter
somewhere out West, and back East was replaced
(if this display of *Early Medical Frauds* regalia is to be credited)
by dozens of suave-tongued colleagues, then *their* dozens:
Golden Orient Powder; Marvel Plasmic Cones; The Deluxe
Mobility and Discomfort Agitator, with Trundle Adjustment;
Dr. Barnhard's Sealing Hood; The Amazing Strato-Lift. . . . And
why not?—where there's hope, there's lying. Where

there's need of any kind, connivery sidles up. I lied
ten dozen times a night in the bar-glow light of being twenty
and lonely and eager for someone's eternal, vow-bound (or simply
imitation) love to save me from the ticking of Oblivion (or anyway
of Boredom), and that lusting fibbing seemed to keep me company
continually; and I was lied to back, by her and her and her
a hundredfold: their own hormonal confusions and greeds. Our hurts
catscradled the air. But of course that matters and it

doesn't matter—after all, we were twenty then, perhaps
we were fifteen then, we were elastic, guys could pop a high one
over the bleachers into the eye of the sun, and girls could sense
the planet calibrate its axis by the perfect teeter-totter

in their implacable bikinied hips. God was in the spring air.
Just to breathe was an aphrodisiac. Sleeping, waking,
made a dotted line we signed. We were going to live forever!
That was Life's guarantee to us.

Universal Elsas

While zooming across the rooftops of Istanbul on a motorbike, [James]
Bond isn't wearing sunglasses at first, then he is, then he isn't!
National Enquirer on the movie **Skyfall**

Plus the blooper with the scarf, and the ones
with the clip-on earrings, the ankle boots, the purse,
the cracked (then not) escape Jeep's windshield.
With a skillion-dollar budget and enough spent joules
of energy to heat an Alpine village for a year,
you'd think there might have been a continuity editor

as capable as Elsa, who commanded every yarmulke
and canapé at my sister's wedding, and certified that the bouquet
for the formal photography session (that wilted)
matched the second bouquet that was carried
down the aisle bloom for bloom and fern for fern.
It's all a matter of some universal Elsa-spirit

overseeing viably—or not. As here, on *this* side of my sister's
chemotherapy—the fatality-cells successfully poisoned
out of her breasts; her hair at last reclaiming
its dominion; and her so-called sense of humor
annoyingly back—the rift in dailiness
seems bridged for now. Not so with Peggy Rabb,

or Mike Anzaldua, or Jake, or Scott: whoever
they were, that "they" has abandoned their bodies,
and on our side of the lymph nodes or the heart or the heroin-weakened chest
that failed, there's no link that even the Grandest Vizier
of the Elsas can fling into nullity-space to watch
catch surely onto an edge and hold. Although if you asked

an ancient Egyptian, you'd learn that after the underworld voyage
in the Afterlife Boat and the Judgment of the Feather of Truth,
the going-on went on: the Nile river geese were netted

in death the same as in life, the spearmen marched,
the lover unfastened her veil, and her unguents were stoppered
into their dainty jars the same as in life—as if

the transition were simply that of the self through new cell
after new cell, in the great unerring wave of replacement
always passing through us. If the feel of a movie blooper
ever troubles me, it's when my father suggests do this
or that, my mother calls me as dusk comes on, and
then, *ka-whang*, I realize they're dead: my inner

Elsa's missed a nano-beat. It's no exotic
megavoltage Bond spree, but a not dissimilar trail
of telltale glitches appears: the dog is here, then
isn't; the car gets washed, but later it's dirty;
the click of a door, the drip of a faucet,
the sound of a child quietly crying at night.

This Bookmark

We know that everybody generates a ghost.
What's less well known is that every *self*
has a ghost. Your infant self:

a ghost like a hazy, airborne, snipped-off
foreskin. The ghost of your stupid youth
is forever vomiting out of the passenger side

of the spectral car the ghost of your stupid friend
is driving too fast. Of course the ghost of before
your divorce, your conversion, your night with the men

from outer space, your . . . [fill-in-the-blank].
The astronaut, retired now, still sometimes
sees herself in zero-g, a self that floats

around her current body like mist
around a spindle. Does the diamond see
a tiny ghost of coal? I suppose the energy

our lives give shape and order to
is haunted by the chaos it was
in the earliest days of the universe.

This bookmark from the Smithsonian
is made of papyrus; one night I thought
I saw it bob in a current of the Nile.

Community

In Lamaze Room, all of the practicing coaches and coached
—a dozen couples—sway, back and forth,
like great plants stirred by the same winds.
Some are resentful of the circumstances
that dragged them here, while some show a touch
of the glow that one associates with medieval oil paintings
of the blessed entering Paradise, but all of them
are sharing a relaxing and a squeezing and a cheering-on
from the same instructional video series,
all are muscles laboring
in unison toward a shared flex.
                                        In the wing
around the corner and a floor above, my friend X
is alone in himself. His appendix has burst
extravagantly, and his body is little more
than the container in which his gut exploded
poisonously against the walls. He'll live
or not: there's no prevailing forecast.
Not his wife and not his daughter
and not his favorite memorized poets
are here—not *really*, although
the first two visit around the clock
and the latter get quietly muttered.
"No man is an island,"
John Donne said, but when he wrote it, Donne
was not an astronaut-(himself)
who was tethered loosely to the mother-ship-(himself)
by a leash of toxic-shit-(of-himself)
and floating floating
through the dark of the universe-(himself).

———————

We have no word for joy
in a bird, and can't imagine the joy that travels
so rapidly it's nearly simultaneous
in the group-mind of a migrating flock
—no word for what's,
translated into human language, pure and simple
joy in the accomplishment of being
in a vee, as if the molecules
of a spearhead could delight in the flight
of their mineral alignment.
                              And yet
a straggler goose, an odd-number outlyer,
often serves to remind us
that the sky holds *this* possibility too.

—————————

When my friend X is released
and completes his poem on the experience,
he posts it on his blog.
857 people
"like" the poem on its first day up.
And still . . . as a week of rereading gallumphs along,
a few secede from that union.

—————————

The lecture is in the Community Building,
the topic is "Community! Equality! A Unified Voice!"
—but only one person can fit at the lectern,

separate from her audience.
                              One speaker.
A single queen for the hive.

She's like the person, the astronaut
out on a "space walk,"
fixing a loose part,
while the other voyagers nervously watch
on console-cams in the viewport
as a connection is kept—but barely—
by the squiggling high-tech umbilicus.
                                        And the young man
three rows up from me . . . isn't really, *really* even
in this building. He's awareness-units
streaming through the screen of a handheld info-cloud device
I call the immersiverse.
He may be one of 857 people
liking a poem, but that
—or whatever/wherever he is—isn't happening
here in his body, here in this room,
with the other sixteen of us.

———————

On rare occasions we come a across a dead bee
on the sidewalk, like some small part accidentally fallen
out of a bag from the hardware store. It became
divorced from the hive—and so it died. That
was a term they used in seventeenth-century settlements
here in America, when an adulterer or a witch or someone
who lisped or violated the Sabbath was harried away to live
(and therefore die) in the wilderness
—"hived out." One year later, someone might come across
a skeleton in the leaf-mould, with a blood-red flower growing out
of the ribs as if from the heart.
                                        And yet . . .
and yet to be the outlyer goose!

The life-long wonder it must have been,
to be Einstein!—(or fill in your own example,
lunatic or sane) afloat within clear sight
of the rest of us, but in a transparent bubble
of special knowledge. *I know the secrets of Time.*
I know what the stars sing, like whale to whale.

———————

Those last two lines are from X's poem.
And there's more.
                    When death
is in you like that, a cold probe
up your middle, it's as if you've been entered
by ice from the mountains of Pluto,
and you orbit Pluto, you face away
from the Earth and you stare with ice-eyes
toward Infinity.
                    And more,
much more; but finally
luck and cutting-edge medicine reeled him back
from outer space, intact,
to that wing in a hospital in Virginia,
to a room full of strangers
                              he needs to relearn
as family and friends.

———————

"Push! Push!" the husband yells,
the way he learned to do at Lamaze.
And (every time, it's amazing) a person
appears, a person is suddenly here
in everyone-space, from one-space.

Lack Thoughts

The warrior was a symbol of martial strength, molded from terra cotta and buried more than 2,000 years ago with China's first emperor to defend him in the afterlife.

The statue was helpless, however, against a man in a green sweater and a Phillies hat who, authorities say, sneaked into a closed-off area during a party at the Franklin Institute in Philadelphia in December, put his arm around the statue and took a selfie, and then broke off and stole its thumb.

New York Times

Zachary's son—he's twelve—is traveling to Dallas to have his right leg amputated just below the knee. The entire family, five of them, is going: the psychologist says this is important for his mental well-being. They must think that a part of his mind in the shape of his right-leg-just-below-the-knee will disappear at the same time. There will be that tiny cavity in the center of his self-image, and the breath of grieving will place its mouth on that open—that negative—space, the way the emptiness in an ocarina works . . . will place its mouth there, and will play a doleful, haunting song.

What are we, when divorced from our context? Whatever "our context" is. Religion? Family? Nation? Gender? Poetry, I'd say for myself.

Removed from its body, that terra cotta thumb might look no different than a squatty length of dung—a hardened turd. We'd never know that once it helped to hold the terra cotta reins of an impressive foursquare terra cotta horse nearby an imperial grave.

Not that, I suspect, the universe ranks—hierarchs—the infinite combinations of its atoms here on Earth. The maggot: atoms. The bird of paradise: equally atoms.

———————

A dead bird near the leaf mould, a jay. All of it intact, except for a single missing wing—you can tell the bird died with this wing outstretched—already decomposed, gone into some other existence ahead of the rest.

Maybe in the sky of that "other existence" a single wing is flying, making its way to who-knows-where.

Maybe along the highway below this wing, a single unattached thumb the color of terra cotta is moving through the air, attempting to hitch a ride, ahead of the rest of its body . . . attempting to hitch a ride to who-knows-where.

———————

Statues from the ancient world: how much we can conjecture from just the feet, or just the indication of feet, left on the marble bases of the vandalized ones! He must have been slightly knock-kneed. She jutted her left hip forward, sassy and unashamed. Having studied this specimen from-the-knees-down, we believe he was an archer, with his arrow nocked and keening almost audibly for release, with the weight of his quiver counterbalanced by a swivel of the waist; he may be the one from the epic poem, whose eye is called "hawk-accurate."

Maybe the ones with missing torsos are the best: because we can read our own best into them, and infinitely so. It's what blank space allows. *If only we'd worked at it harder, and healed the marriage . . . we'd be on a tropical beach now, sipping our costly coco locos from their hollowed shells; you'd jut your hip at me; I'd master your furies with the glare of the hawk.*

This is what attracts us to Sappho's fragments. Not that her writing—her actual words we've been lucky enough to save from time—isn't what we demand of a talented literary singer. The longing; the gaiety; the dialogue of palm and slope-of-breast; and all of the rest.

But it's the vanish-space shot through these and around these, that beckons—that hums with the possibilities we can provide. The way the investigators on cop shows these days belabor the minimal scrapings under a fingernail; or next week's show, a loosened thread from a fragrant eighteenth century leatherbound binding.

A portrait eventually emerges from these.

Sappho scholarship is imagination, love—and forensic science.

———

I think of that recent physics (or for me it's *beyond* my under-standing of "physics") experiment: two "entangled" photons (or was it protons?—see what I mean?), one remaining on Earth, and one delivered into orbit *around* the Earth, but keeping their intertwined association alive. Their familial bond.

It's why I have no pittance of empathy for Michael Rohana, egotist, bozo, destroyer.

The thumb in a drawer of his bedroom bureau, with a wriggle inside it, it can't release; a longing mewl inside it, it can't let out. Entangled over time and space with a terra cotta hand on the terra cotta body of a cavalryman, one of ten on display in a hall of now ninety-nine terra cotta fingers.

Like anybody, any thing, that helps brake the speed of the universe as it flies apart . . . this thumb, too, yearns for union. It dreams—as the hand must dream—of restoral.

———————

In the strictest interpretation of Jewish orthodoxy, a body that's been damaged or altered in any way is unburiable in the holy ground of a Jewish cemetery. At least that's the wisdom I remember being current in my childhood. If it's modulated by now for a generation of Jews with piercings and tattoos and saline mega-boobs and Botox, I don't know.

But I know that only a Heaven devoid of any charity would turn its back on Zachary's son. And what were the funerary laws of sanctity in ancient China, when an emperor was buried along with his statuary bodyguards? It's possible, maybe it's likely, that the "real life" soldier the artisans used as a template for the upright afterlife bodyguard on display in Philadelphia—a cavalry soldier, young and fierce and proud— *was* shorn of a thumb, was a warrior who may have been battlesavaged in a dozen ways. Surely the artisans saw that he was cosmeticized toward physical perfection, in acknowledgment of his duty to serve the Perfect One until the end of time.

If we could conjure him back across the intervening 2,000 years of dust—to testify, let's say, in the trial of Michael Rohana of Delaware, 24 (the jerk), who was charged with "theft of an artwork from a museum"— is it possible he'd raise a hand while taking his oath that shows us how, with missing thumb, his terra cotta avatar is now, in the wake of Rohana's theft, *more* accurate to his lived self?

And it might be more than a thumb, of course. Would he open the hole in his "real life" face as we sit in the courtroom watching him, and suggest by this that the statue of him would be more realistic if someone chiseled the terra cotta right eye out of its terra cotta head?

————————

Joan Whisnant was born without arms in Oklahoma in 1924. "At six, she could write, eat from her plate with a knife and fork, drink from a glass, cut paper dolls, embroider." Eventually she learned the guitar. "She married, and had a baby in 1947 . . . her dexterous feet had no difficulties changing diapers." I was about to say how well she adapted to armlessness, but of course the point is she didn't "adapt": she was *always* her self, she defined her own base-level normalcy.

The same is true of Prince Randian, the Living Torso, "born completely limbless." In the movie *Freaks* "he rolls a cigarette with his lips, then lights a match to smoke it. Among his other skills were painting, shaving, shooting marbles, and writing with his lips. . . . He and his wife had five children." Not once in this book of sideshow performers is there any sense of bitterness or self-pity, despite the visual weight of absence that surrounds them, like a nimbus of active nothingness, in their photographs.

Jeanie Tomaini was "born without legs, and measured four feet, six inches as an adult." She's being proudly held up in the photograph by husband Al Tomaini, "who was eight feet, four-and-one-half inches." It looks like a product endorsement for half-size people. Their daughter remembers, "Our home life was wonderful: no talk of divorce, no big fights, no drinking, no smoking. Just a family."

Let me not forget the famous photo of Eli Bowen (legless, and so steering the tandem bicycle) and Charles Tripp (armless, so pedaling). They're nattily dressed, in their early 1900s way, and clearly having a pleasant, show-offy time as they pose in the middle of their outing. Again, I want to praise the accommodation they've made—to the bicycle, to everyday life in general. And again: a smallness comes over me. In front of their casual ease, in the face of their expertise and comfort . . . it's we out here, we whole ones, who need to "accommodate" to the standard they set.

The decathalon runner: atoms. Eli Bowen and Charles Tripp: equally atoms.

And yet these sideshow attractions I've just recounted were born that way. They never had some part of themselves *removed*, which is to say they were never left with the nerve-end memory of having possessed it once . . . which, after all, is a different kind of lack. They never experienced that condition where the body's electrochemical self still tingles, pins-and-needles-dancing uselessly inside the stump, as it goes through the effort of "moving" a leg or an arm that no longer exists.

When Abby and Dennis split up after ten years of marriage—of soul-twined, mind-meld, work-as-a-unit marriage, at least in its earlier days—she'd sometimes wake up so miserable in the pit of the night, in sweat, in shivering spasms, "that the only thing I could think to do was call his number, to tell him about it. That was the memory still alive inside me . . . to confide in him." Dennis had nights like that too.

In terms of Zachary's son in Dallas, they had "phantom leg syndrome." Nothing was there, but the old, familiar signals kept going out anyway.

———————

I'm sorry, but . . . everything's going to end. Everything. Aren't I the one who wrote one tick-of-time ago that the universe is flying apart? Aren't you the one who nodded inside yourself in agreement, and kept on reading?

Even the monumentally durable bulk of the Pyramids is a study in erasure. New York. Nanobots. Species. Everything's going to end. This knowledge is with us even before the first slap of the midwife or obstetrician.

Still, it's heartening to see pictures of the cave art—the bison, the fierce eruption of horses from a crack in the rock, the horned and tailed shaman—painted on those walls as if for eternity, undying. And the hand-shapes of the makers of this art, left there like a signature—a defiance of time. They'd blow a gluey powdery paint through a straw, around the hand that became a stencil, and . . . voilà! *I was here, and this is my proof!*

The Sphinx is being rubbed away. The ocean is lapping at California. Ozymandias, etc. Once, a hundred sensibility-lifetimes ago, I had the dream that my writing would endure beyond my own lifetime. But the cultural value of that kind of reading is on the wane, and so is the cultural value of the "profile" I present to the current literary world. I don't mean to kvetch here, but simply to face the truth. My work will be turning to powder.

It turns out many of those hand prints on the cave walls are missing a thumb. That's no surprise; those were perilous times.

Well, let the powder of this piece, this thing called "Lack Thoughts," serve, for its moment, to preserve the fragmentation of Zachary's son and of the terra cotta warrior, in a way that does them (maybe that does all of us, in our varying up-and-down degrees of human breakage) recognition and honor.

AUTOBIOGRAPHY: 1947 / 2018

How Biography Works

_Though today almost forgotten outside academia—at least in the English-
speaking world—Alexander von Humboldt's ideas are still shaping our thinking.
And while his books collect dust in libraries, his name lingers everywhere from
the Humboldt Current running along the coast of Chile and Peru to dozens of
monuments, parks, and mountains in Latin America, including Sierra Humboldt
in Mexico and Pico Humboldt in Venezuela. A town in Argentina, a river in Brazil,
a geyser in Ecuador and a bay in Colombia—all are named after Humboldt._

  _There are Kap Humboldt and Humboldt Glacier in Greenland, as well as
mountain ranges in northern China, South Africa, New Zealand, and Antarctica.
There are rivers and waterfalls in Tasmania and New Zealand as well as parks in
Germany and Rue Alexandre de Humboldt in Paris. In North America alone four
counties, thirteen towns, mountains, bays, lakes, and a river are named after him,
as well as the Humboldt Redwoods State Park in California and Humboldt Parks in
Chicago and Buffalo._

Andrea Wulf, _The Invention of Nature:_
Alexander von Humboldt's New World

And now it all disappears,
it turns to mist in my head
and the mist itself grows thin
and vanishes.
                    Even
when the friend he makes
among the jungle tribesmen
shly reveals the second-best delicacy
is the palm-meat from a certain monkey . . . "What then
is the best?" he asks as a natural follow-up question,
and his informant demurs from making this
admission in language, but slowly
opens Humboldt's loosely fisted hand and,
moving with the clarity of an architect's pencil,
his forefinger outlines
Humboldt's human palm . . . yes, even
                                        that
amazing moment shimmers, breaks apart,
and evaporates. And when
                        he traps,

and then experiments upon, the electric eels
infesting the shallow pools of Calabozo
(five feet long, and delivering shocks of *over
600 volts*), dissecting them, testing the vigor
of conductivity through his body by holding an eel
in one hand, a metal plate in the other
("unsurprisingly, by the end of the day
Humboldt . . . felt sick and feeble"), even

that

astonishing episode ripples, loses its shape
like light on a choppy lake, and never re-coheres,

and

so even
        in discovering the magnetic equator;
and Inca temples; and climbing
the cone volcano Cotopaxi ("appeared so smooth
. . . as if a wood turner had created it
on his lathe"); and visiting Jefferson
in early, mud-holed Washington, D.C.; and one day
stumbling upon a thicket-hidden jaguar; and
the close call with death from curare; and
the hurricane at sea ("the captain's cabin
was flooded so high that they had to swim
through it"); and climbing Chimborazo
along the *cuchilla* ("knife edge") only two inches wide,
to over 19,000 feet, hands numb,
feet bleeding, gums bleeding, and yet
ecstatic over the measurements he could take
with his brass instruments; and the beauty he found
everywhere, the ruby beauty of hummingbirds
"that could rest in a thimble," the showering beauty

of meteors—thousands!—across the night
"as if Heaven's armies were plummeting";
$\qquad\qquad\qquad\qquad\qquad$ all of that,
all of that fades, as suddenly I remember the man
who will be my father, proposing to the woman
who will be my mother, the two of them
in a rowboat on Chicago's

Humboldt Park lagoon.

Do you hear me, world! I'm saying
Irving Goldbarth is attempting to keep his balance,
dropped to one knee in a rented rowboat
as skittish as a colt, as Fannie Seligman
swats mosquitoes and her lower-lower-middle-class
appraising gaze drinks in this man
and his sweet and flamboyant and clumsy
theatrical gesture, and all of the
$\qquad\qquad\qquad\qquad\qquad$ boa constrictors
and river dolphins and tapirs and flamingos
and crocodiles and spoonbills and howler monkeys
and titi monkeys and albatrosses
and hummingbird-eating spiders and vicuñas
and slumbering capybaras looking
like molten ingots in the gold
of the jungle riverbank dawn

are washed clean out of my caring by a torrent
of the personal.

Ridiculous Trade

1.

On the washline in the yard,
the flimsies caught in an afternoon breeze
perform veronicas, like capes in the *corrida*
—as if they understand

the world, with its forces and elements,
is always ready to charge against
our little, susceptible lives

—————

etc. It went on, as I remember,
for a number of lines; it wasn't too shabby
a metaphor at all. Where is it now,
among the scraps of notes, the *mulch*
of scraps of notes, that form a history
of long lost opportunities, that weight my past
like lead—the weight
of paper-in-accumulation we always find so surprising.

And the comic "Adventures
of Lame Duck and Cooked Goose" . . .
effluvia now, if even that. The ghost
of the unfinished poem that posits our problems
begin with the stunted dialogue
between our neocortex and our brain stem . . .
I can hear it, some nights, moaning
for release; it wants to leave this world,
but first requires completion.

I was young. I wanted them all
to be "great"—whatever that is.
I wanted the people I loved to be
undying in them. I wanted poems
created of blood, displayed in halls of alabaster.
I was young, I thought that poems should fly
through the heavens like trumpeting seraphs.
Is that so wrong a dream? But where
is that ambition now? In the yard,

the cabbage moths are flying
against the breeze:· for them, on their level,
this might be as heroic—as epic—as anything.

2.

Rural Vermont and New Hampshire. In summer
the hills are such a continuous green,
the boughs look like above-ground tufts
of a single community linked at the roots,
green—that is to say, life—on display
unbroken over hundreds of miles. And yet
the tourists show up on their pilgrimages
(and many of the locals are more abundant too)
in autumn,

when the death of it all
transforms these trees—golden,
umber, amber, cardinal red, deep orange—
into flambeaux; autumn,

when you can see the leaves
hug their immolation
into their bodies. Their loss . . .
their terrible self-burning. . . . *This* is the beauty
we most fervently respond to!—the one
where they seem human.

———————

The poem of David Wojahn's
where he mourns the death of his first wife
Lynda Hull—herself a poet
of consummate blade-sharp skills—
is like a bull that he's dragged
(inside of himself) for decades, and wrestled
onto an altar surrounded by ritual candles
(inside of himself) (the candles rendered
from his own flesh, and their wicks his own
exposed nerves), and then sacrificed
on embers there, to the terrible gods of memory
(inside, inside, inside of himself)
—is a great poem. "Howl"

is a great poem; how much suffering
did its muse and subject, Carl Solomon,
have to endure both in and out
of the booby hatch for Ginsberg to fashion
his poem of angry despair
from those grievous materials? What
enormity of perceived oppression preceded
Adrienne Rich's "Diving into the Wreck"? Or
Akhmatova, Mandelstam . . . I don't think the knock

of the secret police on the door, the brutal clubs,
the journey while hooded, is enough to make
a piece of writing "great": and yet
the fact still is, the knock, and the clubs, and the hood
are part of the dark, dark web of some poems'
dark gestation. Of course there are poems by Kenneth Koch

I'd say are great, that are unashamedly merry;
their *métier* is cheer. *Of course*—as if greatness
and happiness needed to be in conflict!
Still, the brain inside Kafka is closing, opening, closing
itself, tormentedly, like a fist; and Christopher Smart
is on his knees in the street, hosannaing songs
of joyful praise even as his mind is being declared
unfit for the public light. Because

so often the night is longer than even
our most resilient and strenuous hope.
Because the pain in a single cell
of our bodies can be unpacked
and fill the whole of the Lakers stadium.
Because. Because *the world, with its forces and elements,*
is always ready to charge against
our little, susceptible lives.

3.

Once I was engaged to a woman
who'd spent time in . . . well, what I called,
a little above, "the booby hatch"—an easy, awkwardly

comic, term for a house of haunted sleeplessness
and skulls filled with gibbering ghouls.
Her poems about it weren't exceptional; but
is it true: if they ever *would* have been, they'd need
to start in such a house—whether real or metaphor—
and experience its disfiguring hurts?

And me? I've written about her difficult odyssey
through madness, what it took
to exit at last from its gates.
Should I feel uniquely privileged
to have heard her story so intimately? Or

guilty, to have felt its heat
but not to have had my own skin seared
and blistered by being *in* that heat?

————————

Today I'm reclining in bed
with my head on Skyler's butt, while she's
pingponging attention between
some solitaire game and some scary movie
on what I call her squawkscreen, and I'm
idly reading a book on the generation
of America's founders, wondering
why more of its facts won't permanently
stick in my head. It's a simple day

in my seventieth year, a "nothing day," and really
barely worth recording. But I love this woman
and (*knock on wood*) the relative luck

that's beached us here through storms
that have undone others . . . and I wouldn't trade this
(would I?) for the clanging
and unstructuring and restructuring
forge of tragedy that so much of the art I love
seems to have been beat upon,
to a thin, sharp shine.
(Would I?) That's a ridiculous trade, and

please, if there are Fates: then Fates, please
save my life from great poems, oh
I was foolish in my youth when I thought I desired them,
when I believed I wanted their fiery brand
to burn the dearest of names in the lining of my gut, but
no, please let me move complaisantly into the future,
barricaded from unutterably
incinerating power, let me understand the shadows
without being clutched to the breasts of the shadows, oh
please save me from being consumed to the bone,
save me from being consumed to the bone
in the flames of that dangerous excellence.

CODA

There Are 26 Bones in the Human Hand (or Is It 27?)

and not one in the brain.
Unless the brain is *thinking about* the human hand,
as yours is now, and then it too
contains the entire gorgeous fan
of hand bones—imagistically; the way
a typewriter does, when it produces *hand*;
or a laptop screen, when it produces the picture
of a hand (or of a typist typing *hand*,
which then makes three hands).
Once a *typewriter* was the person,
not the machine, and the same
for *computer*: imagine those rows of women
crunching (as we'd say it now) the stats
the big astronomer boys above
relayed to their domain below:
in the blur of black-and-white photography,
how could they not—their dun hair bunned,
their anciently quaint skirts sweeping the floor—
look grayly dowdy, and yet only God knew more
about the stars. Their hands
would deftly tell those astral beads
like a rosary or an abacus, times
a thousand. Today, "computer/woman" likely
implies some futuristic cyborg vamp *so* digital
in her purely pixeled existence, we forget the actual
fingers—the five-staved hand—that gave us
(that handed us) *digital*. That's
how far we've already traveled [mutated?]
into the world of human/exohuman symbiosis.
Example (computer/woman again): when
Harper's reporter Walter Kirn tries on the sample hologoggles
at the Adult Entertainment Expo in Vegas, he interacts

with "the 3-D likeness of actor Lexi Belle . . .
just inches away, close enough to touch
with a glowing pair of virtual hands. She
rolls her hips and sways her fleshy torso. . . .
The computer aligns and matches our gazes.
When I take off the goggles and look around the trade show,
it's the people who seem spookily unreal now."
Whatever "people" are in 2016. *Hello,*
I'm Albert Goldbarth's genome-subsidiary
of Albert Goldbarth's holo-primacy. Pleased to meet you.
It's remedying, if briefly, to imagine
the end of the work day in the basement of astronomy,
where those computational women have been laboring,
like dwarves in a mine of gems, to bring us stars
—or at least the knowledge of the spectra of stars—
from darkness; and at home, at last, their real hands
continue to really engage with the planet: someone's
affixing the suction cup of a milk pump
to her breast and repeatedly, faithfully,
squeezing the rubber bulb; and someone's whisking
through page after page of the family Bible, reading
aloud to her sunken-cheeked mother; and someone's
clumsily fumbling in her haste—that has no patience
for one-at-a-time—with a lover's buttons.
"Real"; and yet, to be fair, a pair
of virtual avatar hands, if
they were mimicking those endeavors, might
ignite the same responsive neurological tinder
waiting in the brain. In the future our dictionaries will fail
at a comprehensive entry for "identity."
I'll be taking a gender-modification chip implant

this weekend, with a pseudo-memory upload. . . .
Okay. But for anthropologists Dietrich Stout
and Nada Khreisher (Emory University), "chip"
is manual: the by-hand knapping of flint stones,
hard-won flake by flake, into usable
Paleolithic-lookalike hand-axes ("this is work
requiring powerful blows, accurate down to a focus
of single millimeters"—"last year, the pile of chipped-away
stone residue weighed over 3,000 pounds"). Connected
to magnetic resonance imaging technology, these experts
and their groups of student knappers are exploring
how the brain lights up—a small town seen at night
from the air—in response to specific tool-making skills.
Knap. The supramarginal gyrus.
Knap. The right inferior frontal gyrus.
Neuromapping the link between this Stone Age talent
and the development of language. It's true,
sometimes when I take my wife's hand into my own
it's almost like speech, a nonverbal speech,
and thousands of questions flow up my arm
and into my brain, to the stars, to the stones, collected
in there, to my crazy confusion of multiple selves
our species never stops generating,
bountifully and thrillingly—and frighteningly.
Knap knap.
Who's there?

ACKNOWLEDGMENTS

The author is grateful to the editors of the following publications, where the poems of *The Now* originally appeared:

American Poetry Review: "P. L.," "Change," "Makes the Beauty," "Universal Elsas"; *Boulevard*: "I Never Do Read the Last Chapter"; *December*: "There are poems about paintings, but the paintings are lost."; *Gettysburg Review*: "This Age of Terror," "One Definition of Time," "'John Adams just died,' I announce"; *Green Mountains Review*: "My Friend Dayvon, a Flying Saucer Enthusiast (Read: 'Nut')," "Deep Down," "James Madison as a Humming," "Walt Whitman, Barbara Bath," "Community" (as "857 People"), "There Are 26 Bones in the Human Hand (or Is It 27?)"; *Kenyon Review*: "Wrist Beep"; *New Letters*: "Rhapsody at the End of Human Language," "Album," "Switch," "I'm tired of my student Scott Galloway," "This Bookmark"; *New Michigan Press* (in the chapbook *The World of Multicongruencies We Tend to Inhabit Increasingly*): "g0," "A Talky Trip Through Mash-Up Time"; *Parnassus*: "Fraud."

Some of these poems have also appeared in the anthologies *The Pushcart Prize 2018* and *GET LIT!*, and on the *Poetry Daily* website. Special thanks to Diane Boller and Don Selby.

None of these poems was written, researched, or submitted using computer technology: and the editors of the above publications have earned my extra gratitude for enabling my offline world.